J 641.5943 Par

Parnell, Helga.

Cooking the German way /

cooking the German way

Apple cake *(back)* is a dessert commonly served with afternoon coffee, while **Black Forest torte** *(front)* is usually saved for special occasions. (Recipes on pages 41 and 42.)

cooking the
German way

HELGA PARNELL

PHOTOGRAPHS BY ROBERT L. AND DIANE WOLFE

easy menu *ethnic* cookbooks

Lerner Publications Company ▪ Minneapolis

Editor: Vicki Revsbech
Drawings by Jeanette Swofford
Map by Laura Westlund

The page border for this book is based on patterns used in a
form of German folk painting called Bauernmalerie.

To my husband, Frank, who loves German cooking
and encourages me to keep up German traditions

Library of Congress Cataloging-in-Publication Data

Parnell, Helga.
  Cooking the German Way/Helga Parnell; photographs by Robert L.
and Diane Wolfe.
    p. cm.—(Easy menu ethnic cookbooks)
  Includes index.
  Summary: Introduces the history, land, and food of Germany and
includes recipes for such dishes as potato dumplings, noodle salad,
and Black Forest torte.
  ISBN 0-8225-0918-0 (lib. bdg.)
  1. Cookery, German—Juvenile literature. 2. Germany—Social life
and customs—Juvenile literature. [1. Cookery, German.
2. Germany—Social life and customs.] I. Wolfe, Robert L., ill.
II. Wolfe, Diane. ill. III. Title. IV. Series.
TX721.P27 1988
641.5943—dc19   87-36642
                                                      CIP
                                                       AC

Manufactured in the United States of America

5 6 7 8 9 10 – P/JR – 99 98 97 96 95

**Creamed spinach *(front)*, green beans *(center)*, and
red cabbage *(back)* are all made with vegetables
that might be found in a German garden. (Recipes
on pages 30 and 31.)**

CONTENTS

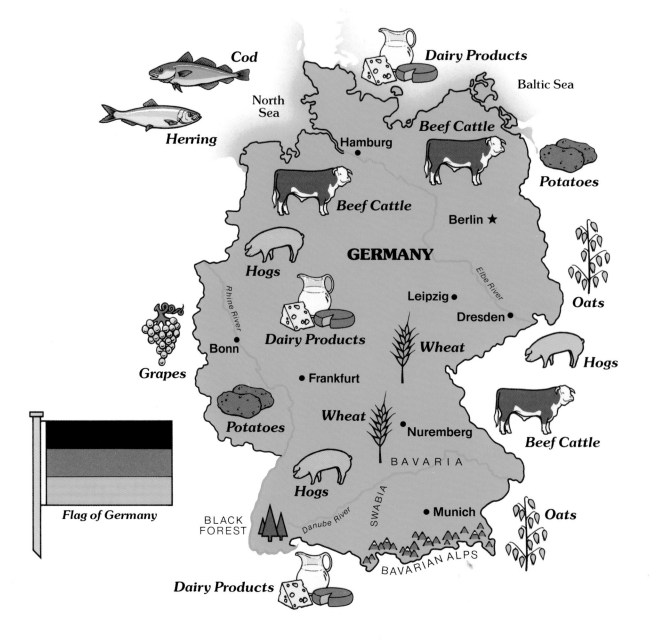

Cod

Herring

North
Sea

Dairy Products

Baltic Sea

Beef Cattle

Hamburg

Potatoes

Berlin ★

Beef Cattle

GERMANY

Hogs

Rhine River

Dairy Products

Leipzig •

Elbe River

Oats

Dresden •

Grapes

Bonn •

Wheat

Hogs

• Frankfurt

Wheat

Beef Cattle

Potatoes

• Nuremberg

BAVARIA

Hogs

SWABIA

• Munich

Oats

BLACK
FOREST

Danube River

Flag of Germany

Dairy Products

BAVARIAN ALPS

INTRODUCTION

With its hearty sausages and roasts, savory dumplings and spaetzle, and rich pastries and tortes, Germany has long been known for its delicious cuisine. Although many of its foods and cooking traditions have remained the same for generations, the country itself has undergone many changes over the years. After World War II, Germany was split into two parts because of political differences. The land became two countries—the Federal Republic of Germany, or West Germany, and the German Democratic Republic, or East Germany. In 1990, the two Germanys became one again.

Germans all have the same ancestors and once shared the same traditions, but during the time in which the country was divided, the two parts grew to be quite different. This book will introduce you to the food and traditions of my homeland in western Germany.

THE LAND

I grew up in the town of Bamberg, which lies just north of Nuremberg in the southern state of Bavaria. Bavaria is a varied land of majestic mountains, winding brooks, and wide, powerful rivers. The Bavarian countryside is made up of small forests and quaint villages and miles and miles of fertile farmland.

The highest point in Germany is the Zugspitze in the Bavarian Alps. A cogwheel train takes visitors all the way to the snow-capped peak of the Zugspitze, 9,721 feet (2,963 meters) above sea level. The view from the train is breathtaking, and in the summer, the passengers can see delicate-looking flowers like edelweiss and alpine rose clinging to the rugged cliffs.

To the west of Bavaria is the Schwarzwald— the Black Forest. This mountainous region is covered with dark forests of evergreen trees. Tradition is strong in the Black Forest, and many of its people still make their living selling the crafts they have made, including toys, musical instruments, and cuckoo clocks.

This picturesque section of Bamberg, Germany, is called Little Venice because the houses are built so close to the Regnitz River.

The Rhine-Main River area in western Germany has such major cities as Frankfurt and Bonn, as well as tiny picturesque villages that seem untouched by modern times. The Rhine River has cut deep gorges into the land, and in many places, castles built on top of the cliffs tower over the water. Central Germany is also fairy tale country. Jakob and Wilhelm Grimm were born near Frankfurt in the town of Hanau. Inspired by the beauty of central Germany, the two brothers made this area the setting for their famous fairy tales.

Northwestern Germany is a low, flat area that borders on the North Sea. There are ports in this region that have connected the Germans with the rest of the world since the 1500s.

Throughout Germany there is a sense of history coming alive. To this day, historic pageants and festivals take place in towns and villages in all parts of the country. Each region has its own special traditions, but everywhere there is a feeling of *Gemütlichkeit*, which is a warm friendliness to both friends and strangers.

A GERMAN CHRISTMAS

Each German holiday has its own traditions to make it special. But of all the holidays, Christmas has always been my favorite.

Every year on the first Sunday of Advent—the Sunday closest to November 30—my family would set out an *Adventskranz*, an Advent wreath. An Advent wreath is a circle of evergreen branches decorated with four red candles—one for each Sunday in Advent. Our wreath was hung from the ceiling with red ribbons or placed in the center of the dinner table. Every Sunday until Christmas, my family would gather to sing Christmas carols as a new candle was lit.

German children sometimes count down the days before Christmas with an Advent calendar. An Advent calendar is a colorful calendar with little doors to open, one for every day in December until Christmas. Behind each door is a little surprise that makes the waiting easier.

In my family, the first week of December was always especially busy. During this time, my mother would do all the Christmas baking.

She made cookies and gingerbread and *Christstollen,* a special Christmas bread. On December 4, St. Barbara's Day, we would set out apple or cherry twigs in a vase of warm water so they would bloom in time for Christmas. Best of all was the eve of December 6. This was the night St. Nikolaus came.

St. Nikolaus has a white beard and dresses like a bishop, in long robes. We believed he had a big book that told him who was good and who was bad. If we had been good, he would leave us gifts of gingerbread, apples, and nuts. If we had been bad, we would promise to try to do better in the coming year.

After a long month of preparation, Christmas would finally come. Christmas Eve was a magical night. Every year, my family would go to midnight mass. As we walked through the streets to the church, the chilly night air would be filled with the sound of church bells ringing, and sometimes the first snow of the season would start to fall. When we returned home from church, we would find that the Christkind had been there while we were gone, leaving presents for everyone and a *Tannenbaum,* a lovely decorated Christmas tree.

The next day, Christmas Day, my family would gather together again for our traditional Christmas dinner. We would have roast goose with vegetables and potato dumplings. Christmas was not over on December 25, for on December 26, friends and relatives would come to talk and eat and admire the tree.

THE FOOD

Germans often talk about *die Kunst des guten Kochens,* which means "the art of good cooking." Cooking is indeed an art in Germany. The most important ingredients a German cook can put into a recipe are love, time, patience, and imagination. To this he or she adds only the freshest meats, dairy products, vegetables, fruits, and bakery goods. The result, whether a simple family supper or a holiday feast, is a delicious meal for friends and family to enjoy.

Although there is a basic German cuisine, there are some regions in Germany that have their own definite cooking traditions. Bavaria is known for its especially hearty meals. Pork roast, served with either potato dumplings or bread dumplings, is popular in nearly every Bavarian home. Even within Bavaria, there are counties with their own culinary specialties. For instance, trout is often served in the Bavarian county of Frankische Schweiz, where ice-cold streams offer an abundant supply of the delicious fish.

In Swabia, a region just west of Bavaria, the specialty is spaetzle, a kind of noodle that can be served with almost any dish. *Sauerbraten* is popular throughout Germany, but in the Rhine River area, cooks add raisins to the traditional recipe. The dish associated with the coal and iron mining region in the north-western section of Germany is a hearty meat and vegetable stew called *Eintopf.* The miners often take *Eintopf,* which means "one pot," to work for lunch because it is an entire meal that is easy to carry and is nutritious and filling.

There was a time after World War II when Germans turned away from traditional German cuisine. To celebrate their recovery from the war years, when food was scarce all over the world, the Germans created a new, very rich style of cooking. It wasn't long, however, before people began to realize that the delicious new dishes were not very healthy. This led to a wonderful combination of the best of both the old and the new styles of German cooking, which can be found in the recipes in this book.

BEFORE YOU BEGIN

Cooking any dish, plain or fancy, is easier and more fun if you are familiar with its ingredients. German cooking makes use of some ingredients that you may not know. You should also be familiar with the special terms that will be used in various recipes in this book. Therefore, *before* you start cooking any of the dishes in this book, study the following "dictionary" of special ingredients and terms very carefully. Then read through each recipe you want to try from beginning to end.

Now you are ready to shop for ingredients and to organize the cookware you will need. Once you have assembled everything, you can begin to cook. It is also very important to read *The Careful Cook* on page 44 before you start. Following these rules will make your cooking experience safe, fun, and easy.

COOKING UTENSILS

colander – A bowl with holes in the bottom and sides. It is used for draining liquid from a solid food.

cruet – A slender glass bottle with a tight-fitting top, used to prepare and store salad dressing

grater – A utensil with sharp-edged holes, used to grate food into small pieces

potato ricer – A utensil in which foods are pressed through small holes to produce strands the diameter of rice grains

rolling pin – A cylindrical tool used for rolling out dough

sieve – A bowl-shaped utensil made of wire mesh, used to wash or drain small, fine foods

slotted spoon – A spoon with small openings in the bowl. It is used to pick solid food out of a liquid.

springform pan – A pan with a detachable rim

tongs – A utensil shaped either like tweezers or scissors with flat, blunt ends, used to grasp food

COOKING TERMS

beat – To stir rapidly in a circular motion

boil – To heat a liquid over high heat until bubbles form and rise rapidly to the surface

brown – To cook food quickly with high heat so that the surface turns an even brown

core – To remove the center part of a fruit or vegetable

cream – To beat several ingredients together until the mixture has a smooth consistency

dice – To chop food into small, square pieces

dust – To sprinkle the surface of something lightly with a substance, usually flour or sugar

fold – To blend an ingredient with other ingredients by using a gentle, overturning circular motion instead of by stirring or beating

garnish – To decorate with a small piece of food such as parsley

grate – To cut into tiny pieces by rubbing the food against a grater

hard-boil – To cook an egg in its shell until both the yolk and white are firm

marinade – A seasoned liquid in which a food is marinated, or soaked

pinch – A very small amount, usually what you can pick up between your thumb and forefinger

preheat – To allow an oven to warm up to a certain temperature before putting food in it

sauté – To fry quickly over high heat in oil or fat, stirring or turning the food to prevent burning

scald – To heat a liquid (such as milk) to a temperature just below its boiling point

shred – To tear or cut into small pieces, by hand or with a grater

sift – To put an ingredient, such as flour or sugar, through a sifter to break up any lumps

simmer – To cook over low heat in liquid kept just below its boiling point. Bubbles may occasionally rise to the surface.

steam – To cook food with the steam from boiling water

whip – To beat cream, gelatin, or egg white at high speed until light and fluffy in texture

SPECIAL INGREDIENTS

almond extract – A liquid made from the oil of almonds that is used to give an almond flavor to food

basil – A rich, fragrant herb whose leaves are used, fresh or dried, in cooking

bay leaf – The dried leaf of the bay (also called laurel) tree

bread crumbs – Tiny pieces of stale bread made by crushing the bread with a rolling pin or the bottom of a glass. Packaged bread crumbs can be bought at grocery stores.

caraway seed – A strong-flavored seed often used in breads and cheeses

chives – A member of the onion family whose thin, green stalks are chopped and used as a garnish and a flavoring

cinnamon – A spice made from the bark of a tree in the laurel family, which is available ground and in sticks

cloves – Dried buds from a small evergreen tree that can be used whole or ground to flavor food

coriander – A sharp-flavored herb used as a seasoning and as a garnish

cornstarch – A fine, white starch made from corn, commonly used for thickening sauces and gravies

croutons – Small cubes of toasted bread

Dijon-style mustard – A commercially pre-pared condiment (ingredient used to enhance the flavor of food) made from mustard seed, white wine, vinegar, salt, and other spices

dill weed – An aromatic herb whose seeds and leaves are both used in cooking

garlic – An herb whose distinctive flavor is used in many dishes. Each bulb can be broken up into several small sections called cloves. Most recipes use only one or two cloves. Before you chop up a clove of garlic, you will have to remove the papery covering that surrounds it.

maraschino cherries – Large cherries preserved in a sweet liquid

mustard seed – The pungent seed of the mustard plant, which is used to flavor food

nutmeg – A fragrant spice, either whole or ground, that is often used in desserts *oregano* — The dried leaves, whole or ground, of a rich and fragrant herb that is used as a seasoning in cooking

parsley — A green, leafy herb used as a seasoning and as a garnish

parsnip — The long, white, sweet-tasting root vegetable of the parsnip plant

peppercorns — The berries of an East Indian plant. Peppercorns are used both whole and ground (pepper) to flavor food.

red wine vinegar — A vinegar made with red wine

rutabaga — The edible, yellow root vegetable of a plant similar to the turnip

semolina — A wheat product that can be eaten as a cereal

slivered almonds — Almonds that have been split into thin strips

soup greens — A combination of vegetables used to flavor soups, stews, and other dishes. To make about ½ cup of soup greens, chop finely and combine one small peeled carrot, four celery tops, one smalled peeled parsnip, and three green onions.

thyme — A fragrant herb used fresh or dried to season food

unsweetened baking chocolate — Solid chocolate usually packaged in 1-ounce squares

vanilla extract — A liquid made from vanilla beans that is used to flavor food

white pepper — Ground peppercorns that have had their hulls removed. White pepper is milder than black pepper.

A GERMAN MENU

Below is a menu plan for a typical day of German cooking. Several alternatives for dinner and supper are given, as well as a list of foods for a festive dinner. Germans generally don't eat dessert after a meal, although fruit is sometimes served. The wonderful pastries for which Germany is famous are eaten as an afternoon snack with coffee, tea, or milk.   *Recipe included in book*

ENGLISH	GERMAN	PRONUNCIATION GUIDE
Breakfast	**Frühstück**	FREW-shtook
Hard Rolls	Brötchen	BROHT-hen
Quark	Quark	KVARK
Soft-boiled Egg	Weiches Ei	VY-kihs EYE
Fresh Fruit	Frisches Obst	FREESH-ehs OHBST
Coffee, Tea, or Milk	Kaffee, Tee, oder Milch	KAHF-ay, TAY, OH-dehr MILKH
Dinner	**Mittagessen**	MITT-ahg-ehs-en
I	I	
*Clear Beef Broth	Klare Fleischbrühe	KLAHR-eh FLYSH-brew-eh
*Pork Roast	Schweinebraten	SHVYN-eh-brah-ten
*Creamed Spinach	Spinat	shpin-AHT
*Potato Dumplings	Kartoffel Klösse	kar-TOHF-el KLOHS-eh
II	II	
*Cod with Mustard Sauce	Kabeljau mit Senfsosse	KAH-behl-yow MITT SENF-zow-zeh
*Tossed Salad with Sweet and Sour Dressing	Grüner Salat	GROON-ehr sah-LAHT
*Parsley Potatoes	Salz Kartoffeln	SAHLZ kar-TOHF-eln
Fresh Fruit	Frisches Obst	FREESH-ehs OHBST

ENGLISH	GERMAN	PRONUNCIATION GUIDE
III	III	
*One-pot Meal	Eintopf	EYN-tohpf
Bread	Brot	BROHT
Festive Dinner	**Festessen**	FEHST-ehs-en
*Clear Beef Broth with	Klare Fleischbrühe mit	KLAHR-eh FLYSH-brew-eh
Liver Dumplings	Leberknödel oder	MITT LAY-behr-k'nohd-el
or Semolina Dumplings	Griessnockerl	OH-dehr GREES-nock-ehr-el
*Marinated Roast or Beef	Sauerbraten oder	SOUR-brah-ten OH-dehr
Rolls in Cream Sauce	Rindsrouladen in	RIHNDS-roh-lah-den IN
	Rahmsosse	RAHM-zow-zeh
*Red Cabbage	Rotkohl	ROHT-kohl
*Green Beans	Grüne Bohnen	GREW-neh BOHN-en
*Spaetzle	Spätzle	SHPETZ-leh
Supper	**Abendessen**	AH-bend-ehs-en
I	I	
*Open-face Sandwiches	Belegte Brote	behl-EHG-teh BROHT-eh
*Potato Soup	Kartoffelsuppe	kar-TOHF-el-soop-eh
II	II	
*Noodle Salad	Nudelsalat	NOO-dehl-sah-laht
III	III	
*Bologna with Rutabagas	Knoblauchwurst mit Rüben	K'NOH-blaukh-vurst MITT ROO-ben
Pastries	**Gebäck**	**geh-BECK**
*Apple Cake	Schlupfkucken	SHLOOPF-koo-ken
*Black Forest Torte	Schwarzwälder	SHVARZ-vehl-dehr KYRSH-tort-eh
	Kirschtorte	
*Deerback Cake	Rehrücken	RAY-rook-en
*Butter Cookies	Frankische	FRANK-ish-eh
	Butterplatzchen	BOO-tehr-pleht-syehn

BREAKFAST/
Frühstück

A German breakfast, which is eaten between 7:00 and 8:00 A.M., is quite small, usually just rolls and coffee or milk. Sometimes, however, eggs or fruit with *Quark*, a kind of cheese similar to ricotta, are served. On Sundays, some people also have a second breakfast. Second breakfast is eaten at about 10:30 or 11:00 A.M. and is made up of something simple like cheese and crackers and apple juice.

DINNER/
Mittagessen

Germans have traditionally eaten their biggest meal of the day—dinner—at about noon. But these days, most Germans work outside of the home, so dinner is served at night during the week, and the noon meal is usually just a sandwich. On the weekends, however, dinner is still served at the traditional time.

Dinner is a hearty meal that usually starts with a soup, especially if it's a festive dinner. This is followed by some sort of meat—most often a roast. The meat is served with potatoes, spaetzle, or dumplings; a salad; and one or two kinds of vegetables. If dessert is served, it is likely to be very light, usually just fruit or a small dish of pudding or ice cream.

Clear Beef Broth/
Klare Fleischbrühe

My family often started Sunday dinner with this delicious beef broth. The meat from the broth can be sliced and served with mustard sauce (see page 29) or horseradish sauce and parsley potatoes (see page 28).

10 cups water
½ cup fresh soup greens (see page 15)
1 medium onion, peeled and chopped
1 bay leaf
1 to 2 teaspoons salt
¼ teaspoon pepper
1½ pounds beef chuck

½ **pound beef bones**
1 **tablespoon fresh chopped parsley or**
    chives
½ **teaspoon nutmeg**

1. In a large kettle, combine water, soup greens, onion, bay leaf, salt, and pepper. Bring to a boil over high heat.
2. Add meat and bones, cover, and reduce heat to low. Simmer 3 to 4 hours. (Do not boil; it will make the soup cloudy.)
3. Remove meat and bones from broth. Save the meat. Carefully pour broth through sieve with another large pan underneath to catch liquid.
4. Sprinkle broth with parsley or chives and nutmeg and serve by itself or with liver dumplings or semolina dumplings (see pages 20 and 21).

Serves 4 to 6

Clear beef broth is a versatile dish that can be served with liver dumplings *(front)* or semolina dumplings *(back)*.

Liver Dumplings/ Leberknödel

Liver dumplings originated in Bavaria, a state in the southern part of Germany.

¼ loaf stale French bread, broken into
     small pieces
8 to 12 ounces beef liver
1 small onion, peeled and quartered
1 egg
1 tablespoon all-purpose flour
2 teaspoons fresh chopped parsley
1 teaspoon salt
1 recipe clear beef broth (see page 18)

1. In a small bowl, cover bread with warm water and let soak for 10 minutes.
2. Squeeze water out of bread. Grind liver, onion, and bread in a meat grinder. (If you don't have a meat grinder, place liver, onion, and bread in a blender and blend for 30 seconds.)
3. In a large bowl, combine ground meat, onions, and bread. Add egg, flour, parsley, and salt and mix well.

4. In a large saucepan, bring beef broth to a simmer over low heat. With clean, wet hands or a wet tablespoon, scoop up balls of dough and drop into broth.
5. Simmer gently, uncovered, for 20 to 25 minutes or until dumplings rise to the surface of broth.

Serves 4 to 6

Semolina Dumplings/ Griessnockerl

Semolina is a wheat product often eaten as a cereal. You can substitute Cream of Wheat® breakfast cereal, if you like.

1 to 2 tablespoons butter, softened
1 teaspoon salt
6 tablespoons semolina
1 egg, beaten
1 recipe clear beef broth (see page 18)
     fresh chopped parsley or chives
        for garnish

1. In a medium bowl, combine butter and salt and stir until creamy.

2. Add semolina a tablespoon at a time, alternating with beaten egg. Stir well after each addition.

3. Let dough stand at room temperature for 30 minutes.

4. In a large saucepan, bring beef broth to a simmer over low heat. With clean, wet hands or a wet teaspoon, scoop up small balls of dough and drop into broth.

5. Simmer gently, uncovered, for 20 to 25 minutes or until dumplings rise to the surface of the broth.

6. Sprinkle with parsley or chives and serve hot.

Serves 4 to 6

Tossed Salad with Sweet and Sour Dressing/ Grüner Salat

This salad can be made with romaine, red leaf, or Boston head lettuce.

1 medium head lettuce washed and torn into bite-size pieces

Sweet and Sour Dressing:

3 tablespoons vegetable oil
2 tablespoons lemon juice
2 tablespoons vinegar
2 tablespoons water
1 teaspoon sugar
1 teaspoon garlic powder
1 teaspoon oregano
1 teaspoon dill weed
   dash salt
   dash pepper

Combine dressing ingredients in a cruet or jar, cover tightly, and shake well. Pour over lettuce just before serving.

Serves 4 to 6

This traditional German meal features a marinated roast called *Sauerbraten* served with spaetzle and tossed salad with sweet and sour dressing.

Spaetzle/
Spätzle

Spaetzle is especially popular in the Black Forest region of Germany. It is usually served in place of potatoes or noodles with a roast as part of a hearty dinner.

1¾ **cup all-purpose flour**
 1 **teaspoon salt**
 2 **eggs, beaten**
 ½ **to ¾ cup warm water**
 2 **tablespoons butter**

Toasted Bread Crumbs:

¼ **cup butter**
½ **cup bread crumbs**

1. Sift flour and ½ teaspoon salt together into a medium bowl. Make a hollow in the center of flour and add eggs and ¼ cup warm water. Slowly stir the flour into the liquid.
2. Stir in remaining water, little by little, until mixture has the consistency of cookie dough. Beat vigorously with a wooden spoon until small bubbles form.
3. Fill a large saucepan half full of water and add ½ teaspoon salt. Bring to a boil over high heat. Scoop up small pieces of dough with a wet teaspoon and drop into water. Cook only enough spaetzle at one time to fill the pan without touching.
4. Boil, uncovered, for 6 to 8 minutes or until tender. Remove from water with slotted spoon and drain in a colander.
5. When all of spaetzle is done, rinse with cold water and drain well.
6. To make toasted bread crumbs, melt ¼ cup butter in a medium frying pan over medium heat. Add bread crumbs and cook, stirring constantly, until golden brown. Remove from heat and set aside.
7. Just before serving, place spaetzle in a medium saucepan with 2 tablespoons butter. Cook, stirring constantly, over low heat until butter is melted. Sprinkle with toasted bread crumbs.

Serves 4

Marinated Roast/ Sauerbraten

Sauerbraten gets its special flavor from a marinade of vinegar, herbs, and spices. The marinade also tenderizes the meat. After World War II, when the only meat available in my country was very tough, my mother would let the Sauerbraten marinate for as much as five days before cooking it.

1 **3-pound top or bottom round beef roast**
3 **tablespoons all-purpose flour**
¾ **to 1¼ cup water**

Marinade:

2 **cups water**
1 **cup red wine vinegar**
3 **bay leaves**
6 **whole cloves**
½ **teaspoon mustard seed**
¼ **teaspoon dried coriander**
1 **large onion, peeled and chopped**

1. Place meat in a large bowl.
2. In a large saucepan, combine marinade ingredients and bring to a boil over high heat. Pour hot marinade over meat. Cover and refrigerate for 2 days.
3. Preheat oven to 475°.
4. Remove meat from marinade and dry with paper towels. Do not discard marinade. Place meat in a large roasting pan and cook for about 30 minutes or until brown on all sides.
5. Add onions from marinade and 1 to 2 cups of the marinade to meat, cover pan with foil, and roast about 1½ hours or until meat juices are brown.
6. Place meat on a platter. Pour meat juices into a medium saucepan. In a small bowl, combine 3 tablespoons flour with ¼ cup water and slowly stir into meat juices. Bring gravy to a boil over medium-high heat, stirring constantly. Remove from burner and add ½ to 1 cup water to make a thin gravy.
7. Slice *Sauerbraten* and serve with hot gravy.

Serves 6

Beef Rolls in Cream Sauce/ Rindsrouladen in Rahmsosse

Rouladen have always been a favorite Sunday or holiday dish in my family.

4 4- by 8-inch slices round steak, ¼-inch thick
1 teaspoon salt
½ teaspoon pepper
4 teaspoons Dijon-style mustard
4 slices lean bacon
½ cup finely chopped onion
1 large dill pickle, cut lengthwise into 4 spears
6 tablespoons all-purpose flour
3 tablespoons vegetable oil
1½ cups hot water
3 tablespoons cream

1. Place 1 slice of meat on a sheet of waxed paper and sprinkle lightly with salt and pepper. Spread 1 teaspoon of mustard over meat, top with 1 slice of bacon, and sprinkle with 2 tablespoons chopped onion. Place 1 pickle spear at the narrow end of the meat and roll up meat around it. Secure meat roll with a toothpick. Repeat with 3 remaining slices of meat.
2. Pour 4 tablespoons flour into a shallow dish. Roll each meat roll in flour until completely covered.
3. In a large frying pan, heat oil over medium heat for 1 minute. Carefully place meat rolls in oil with tongs and cook for about 10 to 15 minutes or until brown on all sides.
4. Preheat oven to 350°.
5. Place meat rolls in a roasting pan, add hot water, and cover pan tightly. Cook for 1 to 1½ hours or until meat juices are brown.
6. Place meat rolls on a platter and set aside. Pour meat juices into a small saucepan and place over medium heat.
7. Slowly sprinkle meat juices with 2 tablespoons flour, stirring constantly. Remove from heat and stir in cream.
8. Pour cream sauce over meat rolls and serve.

Serves 4

Unlike other dumplings, potato dumplings are not eaten with soup. They are usually served with some sort of meat, such as a pork roast.

Pork Roast/
Schweinebraten

The meat juices from this dish can be served as a clear gravy with potato dumplings or bread dumplings.

1 2- to 3-pound pork shoulder or rolled
   pork loin
1 teaspoon salt
½ teaspoon pepper
½ teaspoon garlic powder or 2 cloves
   garlic, peeled and crushed
½ teaspoon dried thyme
1 bay leaf
2 medium onions, peeled and chopped
2 cups water

1. Preheat oven to 475°. Rub meat with salt, pepper, garlic, thyme, and bay leaf. Place in roasting pan with onions.
2. Brown meat in oven, uncovered, for 30 minutes or until meat juices are brown.
3. Add water, cover pan with foil, and cook for another 1½ hours.

Serves 4 to 6

Potato Dumplings/ Kartoffel Klösse

My mother used to make potato dumplings out of raw potatoes. This recipe, which uses cooked potatoes, is much easier but still makes delicious dumplings.

2½ **pounds potatoes (3 or 4 medium)**
  1 **cup milk**
  2 **teaspoons salt**
1½ **cups cornstarch**
      flour for molding dumplings
  ½ **cup unseasoned croutons**

1. Wash potatoes well and place in a large saucepan. Cover with water and bring to a boil over high heat. Reduce heat to medium-low and cover, leaving cover slightly ajar to let steam escape.
2. Cook for 20 to 25 minutes or until potatoes can be easily pierced with a fork. Drain in a colander.
3. Peel potatoes as soon as they are cool enough to handle.
4. Press potatoes through a potato ricer into a large bowl. If you don't have a ricer, grate potatoes through largest holes of a grater.
5. In a small saucepan, scald milk over medium heat.
6. Add hot milk, 1 teaspoon salt, and cornstarch to potatoes and stir well. Set aside for about 15 minutes to thicken.
7. With clean, lightly floured hands, form dough into 3-inch balls. Poke a hole in the middle of each ball and press 2 or 3 croutons into center. Close up holes and reshape dumplings.
8. Fill a large kettle half full of water, add 1 teaspoon salt, and bring to a boil over high heat. Reduce heat to low and, with a slotted spoon, carefully place dumplings in water. Simmer, uncovered, for about 30 minutes or until dumplings rise to the surface.
9. Serve hot.

Makes 6 to 8 dumplings

Parsley Potatoes/
Salz Kartoffeln

*This is a very simple way to prepare
potatoes, a German staple food.*

5 to 7 medium potatoes
½ teaspoon salt
1 tablespoon butter or margarine
2 tablespoons fresh chopped parsley

1. Peel potatoes and cut in half.
2. Place in a large saucepan, cover with
water, and add salt. Bring to a boil over
high heat.
3. Reduce heat to medium-low and cover
pan, leaving cover slightly ajar to let steam
escape. Cook for about 15 to 20 minutes
or until potatoes are tender. Remove from
heat.
4. Drain potatoes in a colander and return
to pan.
5. Add butter and parsley and toss until
butter is melted.

Serves 4 to 6

Cod with Mustard Sauce/
Kabeljau mit Senfsosse

*This dish can be prepared with cod, torsk,
walleye, or any other firm whitefish.*

4 cups water
½ lemon, sliced
1 medium onion, peeled and sliced
2 bay leaves
1 tablespoon fresh soup greens
   (see page 15)
1 teaspoon salt
6 peppercorns
1½ to 2 pounds cod, cut into 4 pieces

1. Place all ingredients except fish in a
kettle and bring to a boil over high heat.
2. Add fish and reduce heat to low.
Simmer, uncovered, for 20 to 25 minutes
or until fish is flaky. Save the cooking
liquid if you want to use it in the
mustard sauce.
3. Serve fish on warm platter with mustard
sauce.

Mustard Sauce:

2 tablespoons butter
2 tablespoons all-purpose flour
1 cup water or 1 cup cooking liquid
  from fish
4 tablespoons Dijon-style mustard
  dash salt
1 teaspoon sugar
1 to 2 tablespoons cream

1. In a medium saucepan, melt butter over low heat. Dust with flour a little at a time, stirring well after each addition.
2. Stir in water a little at a time. Add mustard, salt, and sugar and stir well.
3. Remove from heat and stir in 1 tablespoon cream. Sauce should be creamy and easy to pour. If too thick, stir in another tablespoon of cream.

Serves 4

A rich mustard sauce makes boiled cod a special treat. Serve this dish with parsley potatoes and a tossed salad.

Red Cabbage/ Rotkohl

Red cabbage is served with beef, pork, or wild game, never with chicken or fish.

2 strips bacon, diced
1 medium onion, peeled and chopped
10 to 12 cups shredded red cabbage
1 medium tart apple, peeled, cored, and chopped
4 or 5 whole cloves
2 bay leaves
½ teaspoon salt
⅛ teaspoon pepper
2 teaspoons sugar
¼ cup red wine vinegar

1. In a large saucepan, fry bacon over medium heat until almost crisp. Add onions and sauté until transparent.
2. Add cabbage and stir well. Add remaining ingredients and stir again.
3. Cover and simmer over low heat for 1 to 1½ hours or until cabbage is tender.

Serves 6 to 8

Creamed Spinach/ Spinat

Creamed spinach is a favorite of German children.

2 pounds fresh spinach or 2 10-ounce packages frozen spinach
¼ cup water
3 tablespoons butter or margarine
2 tablespoons all-purpose flour
6 tablespoons cream or milk
½ teaspoon salt
⅛ teaspoon white pepper
⅛ teaspoon nutmeg (optional)
⅛ teaspoon garlic powder (optional)

1. If using fresh spinach, remove stems, and wash and drain well. In a medium saucepan, combine ¼ cup water with a pinch of salt. Add spinach and bring to a boil over high heat. Cover, reduce heat to low, and let spinach steam 5 to 10 minutes or until tender. Drain well in a colander with another pan underneath to catch the cooking water. Save the

cooking water. If using frozen spinach, prepare according to directions on package. Drain well in a colander with another pan underneath to catch the cooking water. Save the cooking water.
2. Chop spinach finely or grind in a meat grinder. Set aside.
3. In a small saucepan, melt butter over low heat. Dust with flour a little at a time, stirring well after each addition.
4. Gradually stir in 6 tablespoons of spinach water. Add cream and spices and stir well.
5. Add spinach and stir. Cover and cook about 15 minutes over low heat or until heated through.

Serves 4 to 6

Green Beans/
Grüne Bohnen

Green beans can also be served cold with sweet and sour dressing (see page 21).

1 to 1½ pounds fresh green beans or 1 pound frozen green beans, thawed, or 1 16-ounce can green beans, drained
6 slices bacon, diced
1 medium onion, peeled and chopped
¼ cup vinegar
2 tablespoons sugar

1. If using fresh green beans, wash well and cut into 1½-inch pieces. In a medium saucepan, bring 2 cups water to a boil over high heat. Add fresh green beans, cover, reduce heat to medium, and cook for 6 to 8 minutes or until beans are almost tender. Drain in a colander.
2. In a large saucepan, fry bacon over medium heat until almost crisp. Add onions and sauté until transparent.
3. Add beans, vinegar, and sugar and stir well. Cover and cook for about 10 minutes or until heated through.

Serves 4 to 6

One-pot Meal/ Eintopf

Eintopf can be made with beef, lamb, or chicken. If you choose beef, use round or rump. If you choose lamb, use shank or shoulder. Either dark or light meat chicken can be used.

1 tablespoon margarine
1 medium onion, peeled and chopped
4 tablespoons fresh soup greens (see page 15)
1 pound meat (beef, lamb, or chicken), cut into bite-size pieces
2 to 2¼ cups water
2 medium potatoes
2 pounds vegetables (any combination of cabbage, carrots, and green beans)
1 teaspoon salt
½ teaspoon pepper
1 medium tomato
2 tablespoons fresh chopped parsley

1. In a large kettle, melt margarine over medium-high heat. Add onion and soup greens and sauté until onion is transparent.
2. Add meat and brown lightly, 10 to 15 minutes. If using chicken, add ¼ cup water.
3. Cover pan, reduce heat to medium-low, and cook until meat is tender, about 15 minutes for chicken and about 45 minutes for beef or lamb.
4. Peel potatoes and carrots and cut into bite-size pieces. Cut remaining vegetables into bite-size pieces.
5. Add 2 cups water, salt, pepper, tomato, potatoes, and remaining vegetables. Cover and simmer over low heat for about 30 minutes or until vegetables are tender.
6. Sprinkle with parsley and serve.

Serves 4 to 6

Eintopf, a hearty meat and vegetable stew, is meant to be a meal in itself.

SUPPER/
Abendessen

On days when dinner is eaten at noon, the evening meal is a very simple, light supper served at 5:30 or 6:00 P.M. Supper usually consists of sandwiches or a hearty soup or salad. Boiled potatoes and marinated herring are also popular.

Noodle Salad/
Nudelsalat

Although this noodle salad can be a meal in itself, it is not unusual to serve it with a small green salad.

8 ounces spaghetti noodles
¼ pound cooked ham, salami, or bologna, cut into thin strips, or ¼ pound weiners, cut into bite-size pieces
¼ pound Swiss cheese, cut into thin strips
1 small red or green pepper, cored and sliced into thin strips
1 medium onion, peeled, cut in half, and sliced
1 large apple, cored and diced
1 gherkin pickle, sliced into thin rounds
1 tablespoon fresh chopped parsley
1 tablespoon fresh chopped chives

Dressing:

4 tablespoons oil
4 tablespoons vinegar
2 tablespoons water
⅛ teaspoon salt
⅛ teaspoon pepper
¼ teaspoon sugar
1 clove garlic, peeled and crushed

1. Break noodles into 3-inch pieces. Cook according to directions on package. Pour into a colander and rinse with cold water. Drain well and pour into large bowl.
2. Add remaining salad ingredients and toss.
3. Place dressing ingredients in a cruet or jar, cover tightly, and shake well.
4. Pour dressing over salad and toss again. Refrigerate at least 1 hour before serving.

Serves 4 to 6

Bologna with Rutabagas/ Knoblauchwurst mit Ruben

1 medium rutabaga, peeled and cubed
1 teaspoon salt
2 tablespoons butter
½ teaspoon caraway seed
1 1-pound ring bologna

1. Place rutabagas in a medium saucepan, cover with water, and add salt.
2. Bring water to a boil over high heat. Reduce heat to medium-low, cover, and simmer about 20 minutes or until rutabagas can be easily pierced with a fork.
3. Drain rutabagas in a colander. Return to pan and mash well with a potato masher or a fork. Stir in butter and caraway.
4. Place bologna in a medium frying pan. Cover and cook over low heat 15 to 20 minutes or until brown and heated through. Serve with rutabagas.

Serves 4

Noodle salad and bologna with rutabagas are two light German suppers that are easy to make.

Potato Soup/
Kartoffelsuppe

Potato soup can be garnished with parsley or sautéed chopped onions.

**6 medium potatoes, peeled and cubed
2 medium carrots, peeled and chopped
2 stalks celery, chopped
1 large onion, peeled and chopped
1 medium parsnip, peeled and chopped
1 ham bone or 1 smoked pork hock
6 cups chicken broth or water
1 teaspoon salt
½ teaspoon pepper**

1. Place potatoes, carrots, celery, onion, parsnip, ham bone, broth, salt, and pepper in a large kettle and bring to a boil over high heat. Reduce heat to low, cover, and simmer 20 to 30 minutes or until vegetables are tender.
2. Carefully pour soup through a large sieve with another pan underneath to catch liquid. Remove ham bone.
3. With a large spoon, press the vegetables through the sieve into soup. You can also mash vegetables into the broth with a potato masher. Stir well.

Serves 4 to 6

Open-face Sandwiches/
Belegte Brote

**4 to 6 slices rye bread
    butter
1 pound cold cuts (salami, bologna,
    ham, or Thuringer)
1 pound sliced cheese (Swiss, cheddar,
    Camembert, Muenster or Colby)
2 to 3 hard-boiled eggs, shelled and
    sliced into thin rounds
1 large red onion, peeled and sliced
2 medium tomatoes, sliced
1 medium cucumber, sliced
    baby pickles (gherkin or dill)
    lettuce**

Arrange ingredients on a large serving plate or on several small plates.

Serves 4 to 6

Open-face sandwiches, which can be plain or fancy, are delicious served with potato soup.

PASTRIES/
Gebäck

Gebäck are the fancy pastries, tortes, rolls, and cookies that are such an important part of German cuisine. These desserts are not served after meals, but rather they are eaten as snacks in the afternoon. At 2:30 or 3:30 P.M., the *Konditoreien*, or coffee shops, are filled with people enjoying such wonderful desserts as Black Forest torte and apple cake.

Deerback Cake/
Rehrücken

Rehrücken *is traditionally made in special pans that are long and narrow, but a loaf pan will also work.*

5 **eggs**
1½ **cups powdered sugar**
1 **cup (6 ounces) ground hazelnuts**
1 **ounce unsweetened baking**
    chocolate, grated
1 **teaspoon lemon juice**

½ **teaspoon vanilla extract**
2 **tablespoons bread crumbs**
1 **cup slivered almonds**

1. Preheat oven to 350°. Grease and flour a 9- by 5-inch loaf pan.
2. Separate eggs, placing yolks in one medium bowl and whites in another. To separate an egg, crack it open over one of the bowls, catching the yolk in one of the eggshell halves and letting the egg white fall into the bowl. Slowly pour the egg yolk back and forth between the two shells, letting the egg white dribble into the bowl, until all of the egg white has been poured off. Be very careful not to break the yolk. Place the yolk in the other bowl.
3. Add sugar to egg yolks and beat until creamy and foamy. Add hazelnuts, chocolate, lemon juice, vanilla extract, and bread crumbs and stir well.
4. Beat egg whites until they form stiff peaks.
5. Fold beaten egg whites into dough until just mixed.

6. Pour dough into 9- by 5-inch loaf pan. Bake for 30 minutes or until toothpick inserted in center of cake comes out clean.
7. Let cake cool in pan for about 5 minutes. Run a knife around the inside of the pan so cake doesn't stick, and turn cake out of pan onto wire rack to finish cooling. Frost when completely cool.
8. Garnish cake with rows of slivered almonds.

Chocolate Frosting:

1½ **cups powdered sugar, sifted**
  3 **tablespoons cocoa**
1½ **tablespoons melted butter**
  3 **tablespoons warm water**

1. Sift powdered sugar and cocoa together into a medium bowl.
2. Add butter and stir. Stir in water, a little at a time. Frosting should be thick and creamy.

Makes about 9 pieces

Deerback cake and butter cookies are two festive desserts that can be served with milk or tea.

Butter Cookies/
Fränkische Butterplätzchen

In Germany, cookies are usually served only at Christmastime. If you don't have cookie cutters, you can use a glass to cut out the cookies.

½ **pound (1 cup) butter, softened**
1 **cup sugar**
3 **eggs at room temperature**
½ **teaspoon vanilla extract**
4 **cups sifted all-purpose flour**

1. In a small saucepan, melt ½ cup butter over low heat. With a spoon, skim off white froth that forms on top of butter and discard. Pour melted butter into a large bowl, leaving behind any sediment that has formed in the bottom of the pan.
2. Add remaining butter and sugar to melted butter and beat until fluffy.
3. Add eggs and vanilla extract and beat well.
4. Add flour, little by little, stirring well after each addition until all flour has been added and dough is smooth.
5. Set dough aside for at least one hour.
6. Preheat oven to 400°.
7. Place dough on a clean flat surface that has been dusted with flour. Dust a rolling pin with flour and roll out dough to ⅛ inch thickness. Cut dough into a variety of shapes with cookie cutters that have been dipped in flour.
8. Carefully place cut-out dough onto ungreased cookie sheets. Bake for 8 to 10 minutes, until edges of cookies just begin to turn brown.
9. While one pan of cookies is baking, gather up leftover scraps of dough and roll into a ball. If necessary, dust rolling surface and rolling pin with flour again. (Don't use too much flour, or cookies will be tough.) Roll out dough and cut into shapes to be baked. Repeat until the dough is used up.

Makes 5 dozen cookies

Apple Cake/
Schlupfkucken

You can substitute one pound of cherries, pitted, for the apples.

1⅓ **cup all-purpose flour**
1¼ **teaspoon baking powder**
¼ **pound (½ cup) margarine, softened**
½ **cup plus 2 tablespoons sugar**
2 **eggs at room temperature**
   rind of ½ lemon, grated
   lemon juice from one lemon
6 **small tart apples**
2 **teaspoons cinnamon**

1. Preheat oven to 350°. Grease a 10-inch springform pan.
2. In a medium bowl, combine flour and baking powder.
3. In a large bowl, cream together margarine and ½ cup sugar. Add eggs and lemon rind and blend until fluffy. Add flour mixture, stir well, and then pour into pan.

4. Squeeze lemon juice into a small bowl. Peel and core apples and cut into quarters. Dip pieces of apple into lemon juice so they won't turn brown as you work with them. Make deep lengthwise cuts in ⅛ inch intervals across rounded side of each piece of apple.
5. Press apples, cut side up, into the dough.
6. In a small bowl, combine cinnamon with 2 tablespoons sugar. Sprinkle evenly over apples.
7. Bake for 30 to 40 minutes or until toothpick inserted in center of cake (not in apple) comes out clean.
8. Serve with whipped cream

Makes 8 to 10 pieces

Black Forest Torte/ Schwarzwälder Kirschtorte

Although this dessert is named for the Black Forest region, many variations of the torte are found all over Germany.

- ½ cup plus 2 tablespoons all-purpose flour
- 1 tablespoon cocoa
- 4 egg yolks (see page 38 for instructions on separating eggs)
- 2 tablespoons warm water
- ¼ teaspoon vanilla extract
- 3 drops almond extract
- ½ cup sugar
- ¼ teaspoon cinnamon
- 3 tablespoons cornstarch
- ½ teaspoon baking powder
- 3 egg whites

Filling and Topping:

- 2 tablespoons cornstarch
- ¼ cup water
- 2 16-ounce cans cherry pie filling
- 2 cups whipping cream, chilled
- ¼ teaspoon vanilla extract
- 1 tablespoon powdered sugar
- ¼ cup grated unsweetened baking chocolate
- 12 to 14 maraschino cherries

1. Preheat oven to 350°. Grease and flour 3 9-inch cake pans.
2. In a small bowl, combine flour and cocoa and set aside.
3. In a medium bowl, combine egg yolks with 2 tablespoons warm water and beat until mixed. While continuing to beat, slowly add vanilla extract, almond extract, and ¼ cup sugar and beat until mixture is creamy. Add cinnamon, flour mixture, cornstarch, and baking powder and mix well.
4. In a medium bowl, beat egg whites while gradually adding remaining sugar. Beat until mixture forms stiff peaks.
5. Fold beaten egg whites into dough until just mixed.
6. Pour ⅓ of batter into each cake pan. Bake for 15 to 20 minutes or until toothpick inserted in center comes out clean.

7. Let cake cool in pans for 5 minutes. Then run a knife around the insides of the pans so cake doesn't stick, and turn out of pans onto wire rack to finish cooling.

8. Make filling. In a small bowl, combine 2 tablespoons cornstarch with 2 tablespoons water and stir until cornstarch is dissolved.

9. In a medium saucepan, bring remaining water to a boil over high heat. Add cornstarch mixture, reduce heat to medium, and cook, stirring constantly, until mixture thickens. Remove from heat.

10. Add pie filling to cornstarch mixture and stir well.

11. In a medium bowl, whip cream until it starts to thicken. Add vanilla extract and powdered sugar and whip until mixture forms stiff peaks. Refrigerate until ready to assemble torte.

12. Wait until layers are completely cool to assemble torte. Place one layer on a cake plate and cover with ½ of cherry mixture and ⅓ of whipped cream. Top with second layer and cover that with remaining cherry mixture and ⅓ of whipped cream. Top with third layer.

13. Frost top and sides of torte with remaining whipped cream and garnish with grated chocolate and maraschino cherries.

14. Refrigerate until ready to serve.

Makes 8 to 10 pieces

THE CAREFUL COOK

Whenever you cook, there are certain safety rules you must always keep in mind. Even experienced cooks follow these rules when they are in the kitchen.

1. Always wash your hands before handling food.
2. Thoroughly wash all raw vegetables and fruits to remove dirt, chemicals, and insecticides.
3. Use a cutting board when cutting up vegetables and fruits. Don't cut them up in your hand! And be sure to cut in a direction *away* from you and your fingers.
4. Long hair or loose clothing can easily catch fire if brought near the burners of a stove. If you have long hair, tie it back before you start cooking.
5. Turn all pot handles toward the back of the stove so that you will not catch your sleeve or jewelry on them. This is especially important when younger brothers and sisters are around. They could easily knock off a pot and get burned.
6. Always use a pot holder to steady hot pots or to take pans out of the oven. Don't use a wet cloth on a hot pan because the steam it produces could burn you.
7. Lift the lid of a steaming pot with the opening away from you so that you will not get burned.
8. If you get burned, hold the burn under cold running water. Do not put grease or butter on it. Cold water helps to take the heat out, but grease or butter will only keep it in.
9. If grease or cooking oil catches fire, throw baking soda or salt at the bottom of the flame to put it out. (Water will *not* put out a grease fire.) Call for help and try to turn all the stove burners to "off."

METRIC CONVERSION CHART

WHEN YOU KNOW		MULTIPLY BY	TO FIND	
MASS (weight)				
ounces	(oz)	28.0	grams	(g)
pounds	(lb)	0.45	kilograms	(kg)
VOLUME				
teaspoons	(tsp)	5.0	milliliters	(ml)
tablespoons	(Tbsp)	15.0	milliliters	
fluid ounces	(oz)	30.0	milliliters	
cup	(c)	0.24	liters	(l)
pint	(pt)	0.47	liters	
quart	(qt)	0.95	liters	
gallon	(gal)	3.8	liters	
TEMPERATURE				
Fahrenheit	(°F)	5/9 (after	Celsius	(°C)
temperature		subtracting 32)	temperature	

COMMON MEASURES AND THEIR EQUIVALENTS

3 teaspoons = 1 tablespoon
8 tablespoons = ½ cup
2 cups = 1 pint
2 pints = 1 quart
4 quarts = 1 gallon
16 ounces = 1 pound

INDEX

(recipes indicated by **boldface** *type)*

ABOUT THE AUTHOR

Helga Parnell grew up in the small town of Bamberg in western Germany, and in 1963, she moved to St. Paul, Minnesota. Since 1969, Parnell has managed the catering, food service, and gift shop for the Volkfest Association, a German culture club. In the hot summer months when she takes a break from the stove, Parnell teaches young children the customs and language of her native land. She also enjoys music, swimming, and cross-country skiing.

Rindsrouladen in Rahmsosse are flavorful meat rolls wrapped around a surprise filling. (Recipe on page 25.)